Baptism Memories & Journal of

I know I am ready to be baptized.
I love Heavenly Father and Jesus.
I want to become more like my Savior,
so I will follow the example Jesus
set when he was baptized in the
Jordan River by John the Baptist.

ISBN 13: 978-1-4621-4143-2

Published by CFI, an imprint of Cedar Fort, Inc.
2373 W. 700 S., Springville, UT 84663
Distributed by Cedar Fort, Inc., www.cedarfort.com

Cover and page design by Shawnda T. Craig

Printed in China

10 9 8 7 6 5 4 3 2

Printed on acid-free paper

MY BAPTISM MEMORIES AND JOURNAL

PIONEER PLUS

MY BAPTISM MEMORIES

AND JOURNAL

My full name is ______________________________

My birthday is ______________________________

I was born at ______________ hospital.

I weighed ________ lbs. and ________ oz.

I was ________ inches long.

My parents gave me my name because ______________________________

____

____

When I am baptized, I take upon me another sacred name,

the name of Jesus Christ.

This means that in all I say and do, I will try

to be like Jesus Christ, my Savior.

My father's full name is ______________________________

My mother's full name is ______________________________

My grandfathers' names are ______________________________

____

My grandmothers' names are ______________________________

____

My brothers' and sisters' names are ________________________

____

____

____

____

When I am baptized, I will become an official member of **The Church of Jesus Christ of Latter-day Saints**!

To become a member of Jesus Christ's Church, I must be *baptized by immersion* by an authorized priesthood holder. I will begin anew with no sins. Then I will be *confirmed* and given the *gift of the Holy Ghost* by the laying on of hands.

Once I am baptized, my name is recorded on the records of The Church of Jesus Christ of Latter-day Saints!

On my baptism day, I make a **promise** to our Heavenly Father—a promise to take upon me the name of Jesus Christ and be a witness of him.

I was baptized by ____

I was baptized on ______________________________
(date)

I was baptized at ____________ o'clock AM PM (circle one)

I was confirmed on ______________________________
(date)

I was confirmed at ____________ o'clock AM PM (circle one)

I was baptized and confirmed in ________________ , ________________
(city) (state / province / territory)

I was confirmed by ____

The witnesses of my baptism were ______________________________

____

____

My Baptism Program

Opening Prayer: ______________________________

Opening Song: ______________________________

Talks: ______________________________

____

____

Musical Number(s): ______________________________

____

Closing Prayer: ______________________________

Family and Friends Who Attended My Baptism

When I was baptized by immersion, I felt

The water felt

When I was washed clean from all my sins, I felt

When the priesthood holders laid their hands upon my head to give me the gift of the Holy Ghost, I felt ______________________________

____

____

____

____

After the confirmation was complete and I had received the gift of the Holy Ghost, I felt ______________________________

____

____

____

____

I prepared for my baptism by ___

___

___

___

___

___

My parents helped prepare me to become a member of The Church of Jesus Christ of Latter-day Saints by ___

___

___

___

___

I chose to be baptized because ______________________________

I was baptized in white because ______________________________

My bishop's name is ______________________________

From my bishop's interview, I learned this about baptism

____

____

____

____

When he said I was worthy and prepared to be baptized, I felt ________

____

____

____

____

____

When I was baptized, the following people celebrated with me

My celebration was held at

We did the following

The following people gave me gifts when I was baptized:

(Include what they gave you)

They gave me the gifts because

A **testimony** is a *special spiritual witness* given by the Holy Ghost. I now have the Holy Ghost and can receive a witness that the Church is true. A witness can be a warm feeling in my heart, a clear mind, or knowing without doubt that something is true. The beginning of a testimony is the knowledge that Heavenly Father lives and loves his children, and that includes me. Heavenly Father loves me! Jesus Christ lives and is the Son of God. This is the beginning of a testimony.

My Testimony

My Testimony

My Dad's Testimony

My Mom's Testimony

Testimonies of My Grandparents

Testimonies of My Grandparents

The best thing about my baptism was

The feeling I remember the most is

Jesus loves me because ______________________________

____

____

____

____

____

I love Jesus because ______________________________

____

____

____

____

____

I am grateful for my dad because ____

I am grateful for my mom because ____

I am grateful for my family because ______________________________________

My Primary teacher's name is ______________________

My favorite Primary song is ______________________

My friends in Primary are ______________________

____

____

____

I like going to Primary because ______________________

____

____

____

____

____

On the following pages are questions that will help you think of things to write about. After answering each question, use the remaining space to write about other things you want to remember.

(date)

My favorite scripture is

Why?

____

(date)

My favorite food is ______________________________

(date)

One of my prayers was answered when

(date)

I am good at

(date)

My favorite friends are

(date)

My favorite Book of Mormon hero is

(date)

Things that I love to do include

(date)

My favorite TV show is

(date)

My favorite ice cream flavor is

(date)

When I get home from school, I like to

____
(date)

My favorite movie is ______________________

(*date*)

My favorite subject in school is

____
(date)

Since I was baptized, I have felt the Holy Ghost when I ______________

(date)

My favorite games to play are

(date)

My favorite colors are

____

(date)

If I could go on a vacation with my family, I would go to ________________

(date)

I am really happy when

(date)

When I read the scriptures, I feel

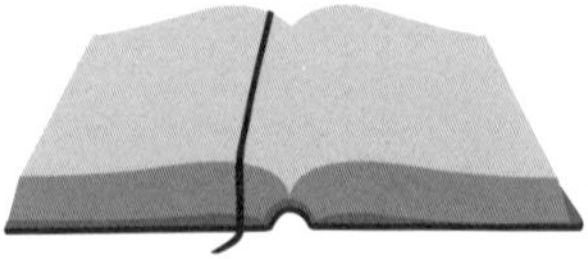

(date)

I love it when my mom and dad

(date)

I don't like to share my

(date)

My favorite thing to do with my family is

(date)

(date)

My friends like me because

(date)

When I pray, I know that Heavenly Father will

(date)

If I could have one wish, it would be

(date)

My favorite candy is

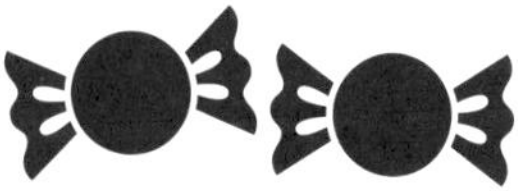

(date)

Today I thought about

(date)

I am missing ______ teeth. I lost one tooth when I ______

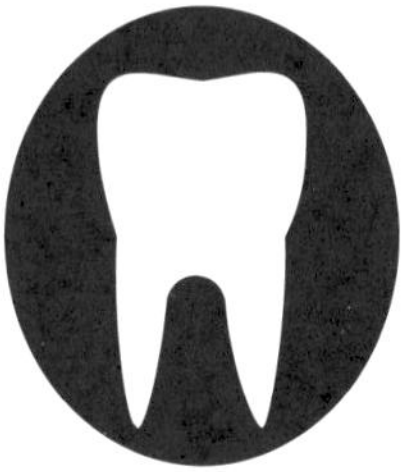

(date)

I can be an example to others by

(date)

I feel sad when

(date)

I know that Heavenly Father loves me because

____
(date)

My favorite thing to do with my grandma or my grandpa is_______________

(date)

I love it when my brother or sister

(date)

My grandma makes me feel special by

(date)

My family is special to me because

(date)

I have a warm feeling in my heart when the Spirit is with me. I have felt the Spirit when I

(date)

I am grateful that I am a member of The Church of Jesus Christ of Latter-day Saints because

(date)

My Primary teacher taught me that

(date)

When I pray, I pray for

(*date*)

(date)

(date)

(date)

(date)

(date)

(date)